Harmonica Primer
with Video & Audio Access

by
Tom Wolf

For Audio & Video Access, go to this address:
http://cvls.com/extras/harmonica/

HOW TO USE

To use the book along with the video, follow these suggestions.

Step 1

Watch a section of the video. Rewind and watch again until you understand the material completely. (A section would be from one title page to the next).

Step 2

Once you understand the section, go to the book to practice the exercises and songs over and over until you are comfortable with them.

Step 3

After practicing with the book, go back to the video and play along to make sure you are performing the material properly.

This course is designed to be worked through, stopping and practicing each section until you are thoroughly familiar with it. It will probably take the average beginning student 2 - 4 months to work all the way through the book and video, so don't rush. Take your time and learn the material correctly.

The information in this book and video combination is the result of over 20 years of studying and performing the harmonica by Tom Wolf, combined with over 60 years of teaching and publishing experience of the Watch & Learn staff. This information was gathered from Tom and organized by Peter Vogl, Bert Casey, and Geoff Hohwald. Peter and Bert in particular spent over 200 hours transcribing, recording, proof reading, and editing the *Harmonica Primer* to make this the finest and most accurate harmonica method available.

INTRODUCTION

The *Harmonica Primer Deluxe Edition* is an instruction book with video & audio access designed for the beginning student who desires a clear, step-by-step method of learning to play the harmonica. Many illustrations are included to make this the easiest to understand course available. The book contains familiar songs in addition to spending much time showing techniques and exercises in order to help establish a firm foundation and background which is necessary in learning to play any instrument.

The video that accompanies this book enables the student to learn 3 or 4 times faster than with other methods. The video provides the accent, tone, and rhythm for all the songs and exercises in this book. You will also be able to see the correct movements of the left and right hand.

THE AUTHOR

Tom Wolf is an Atlanta session musician and Grammy Award nominee. He has over 25 years of experience playing harmonica and has spent many years teaching. Tom also performs regularly around the southeast.

VIDEO & AUDIO ACCESS

For video and audio access to the media in this course, go to this address on the internet:

http://cvls.com/extras/harmonica/

TABLE OF CONTENTS

SECTION 1
GETTING STARTED

For Audio & Video Access, go to this address:
http://cvls.com/extras/harmonica/

PARTS OF THE HARMONICA

Cover Plate

Key

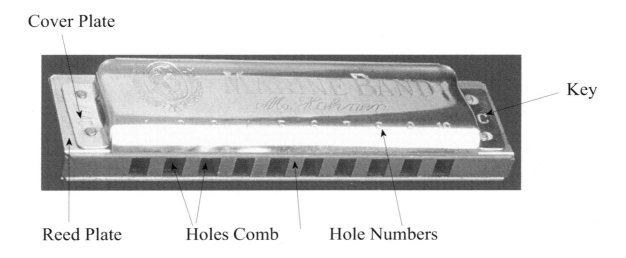

Reed Plate   Holes Comb   Hole Numbers

SELECTING AND CARING FOR YOUR HARMONICA

We will be using a 10 hole diatonic harmonica in the key of C. (The key is stamped on the top of each harmonica). If you have a different harmonica, you can save it to play in different keys later. Unfortunately, state health laws prohibit the return of harmonicas because they are placed on your mouth. If you have any questions regarding choosing your harmonica, your local music store can help.

There are two basic rules in caring for your harmonica:

1. Always play with a clean, dry mouth.

2. When you finish playing the harmonica, tap it out several times to remove any moisture from the reeds.

This is virtually all you need to do to maintain your harmonica (harp for short). Running water through a harp is a risky venture. Although you may unstick an old reed, too much water will make the wood swell, which could hurt your lips. Taking care of your harmonica will make it last a long time.

HARMONICA NOTATION

The 10 holes in the harmonica play one note when you blow and another when you draw. Here are the notes played when you blow and draw.

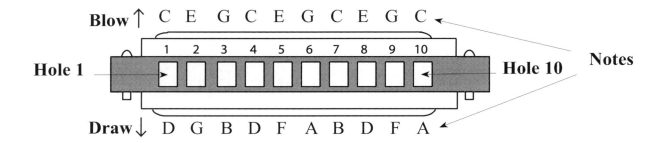

We will be using a number and arrow system to show you when to blow or draw through the harmonica. An up arrow means to blow, think "blowup". A down arrow means to draw air or inhale through the harmonica.

The numbers we use represent the holes in the harmonica. There are 10 possible holes to play through starting numerically from left to right. Hole number 1 is on the far left of the harmonica if the holes are facing you. Hole number 10 is on the far right of the harmonica.

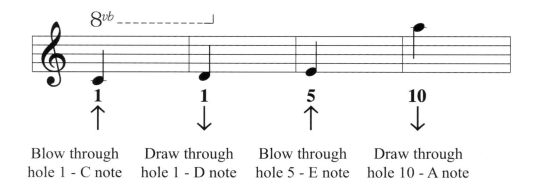

MUSIC NOTATION

○ A whole note gets 4 beats. ♩ A half note gets 2 beats.

♩ A quarter note gets 1 beat. ♪ An eighth note gets half a beat.

THE STAFF

The staff consists of 5 lines and 4 spaces. Each line and space represents a note.

The spaces spell the word: F A C E The lines may be remembered by: **E**very **G**ood **B**oy **D**oes **F**ine

LEDGER LINES

Ledger lines allow us to write notes above or below the staff.

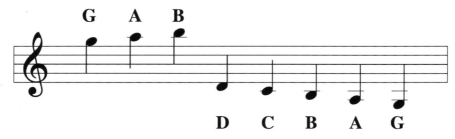

THE CLEF, MEASURES, AND BARLINES

Harmonica music generally uses the treble clef. The staff is divided into measures by barlines.

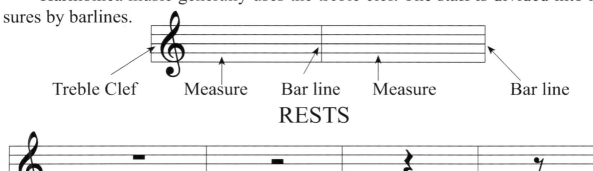

Treble Clef Measure Bar line Measure Bar line

RESTS

Whole note rest Half note rest Quarter note rest Eighth note rest

3

TIME SIGNATURES

The time signature tells you how many beats are in a measure and what note gets one beat.

In 4/4 time or common time, there are 4 beats in a measure and the quarter note gets one beat.

In 3/4 time there are 3 beats in a measure and the quarter note gets one beat.

In 6/8 time there are 6 eighth notes in a measure and the eighth note gets one beat.

DOTS AND TIES

A dot adds half the value of the note it's added to. A dotted quarter note lasts 1 1/2 beats.

A tie connects two notes across a bar line. A half note tied to a quarter gets 3 beats.

8vb

This means the actual notes are played 1 octave lower. Using this allows us to use fewer ledger lines and makes note reading easier.

Using **8vb**   Not using **8vb**

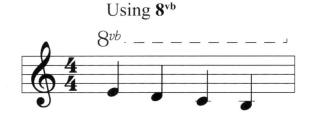 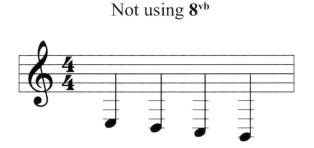

4

HOLDING THE HARMONICA

There are several accepted ways to hold the harmonica. This is what I recommend.

Step 1

With the holes facing you numbered 1 to 10 going from left to right, cup your right hand around the harmonica.

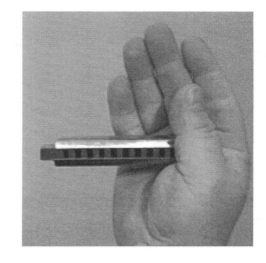

Step 2

Let the left side of the harmonica rest against your left hand with the fingers cupped around the harmonica.

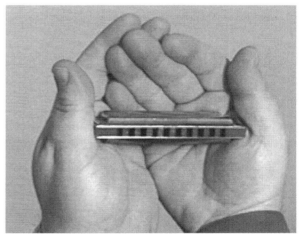

Step 3

Do not block any of the holes with any part of your hand and don't squeeze the harmonica.

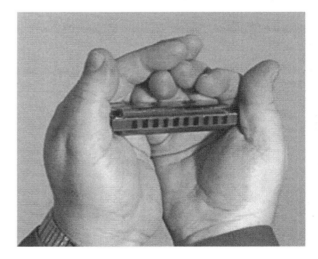

SECTION 2
PLAYING IN FIRST
POSITION

For Audio & Video Access, go to this address:
http://cvls.com/extras/harmonica/

BLOWING

Step 1

Hold the harmonica like we have just learned and bring the harmonica to your mouth and blow. You must shape your mouth around each hole creating a vacuum, not letting air through any place but the hole you are playing. Try to blow into one hole at a time.

Step 2

A good exercise is to take a straw, place it in your mouth, and blow through it. Feel how your mouth is shaped around the straw. That's what your mouth needs to do around each hole. Try sucking in through the straw. This is how air must pass through each hole in the harmonica.

EXERCISE 1

Place the harmonica to your mouth and blow through hole number 1. Remember 8vb means the note sounds 1 octave lower than written.

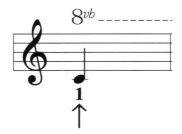

Try to play just one note. A good way to practice this is to place the tip of your tongue against the hole you are playing. Shape your lips around your tongue, withdraw your tongue, (keeping this shape with your mouth) and blow into the hole. This should give you one note. We don't use this technique when playing. This is just to help you get the feel of playing one note at a time.

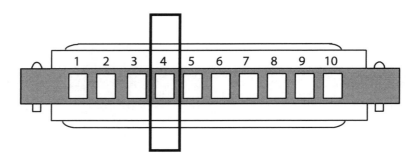

EXERCISE 2

Practice blowing through each hole of the harmonica. Remember 8vb means the notes are played one octave lower than written.

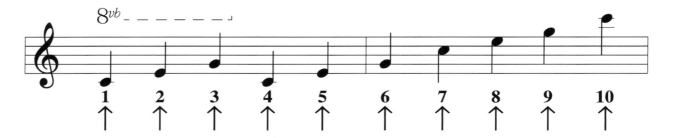

Here is another way to practice playing one note at a time. Place your thumbs over the holes on both sides of the hole you intend to play, blocking those holes. Now place your mouth up to the harmonica, positioning it over the hole you intend to play. Now remove your fingers and play. Practice playing one note at a time until you sound like the Video.

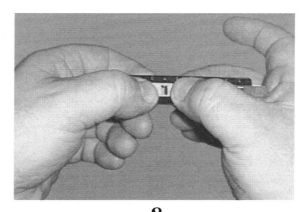

DRAWING

EXERCISE 3

Draw or inhale through each hole.

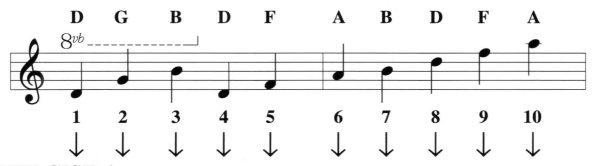

EXERCISE 4

Blow through holes 1 through 4, then draw through each hole coming backwards. Practice this until you can play each note without making more than one sound at a time.

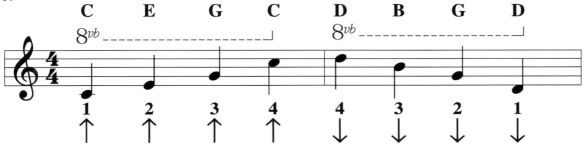

THE C MAJOR SCALE

EXERCISE 5

We will now learn how to play a major scale on the harmonica. This is a C Major scale since we are using a C harmonica.

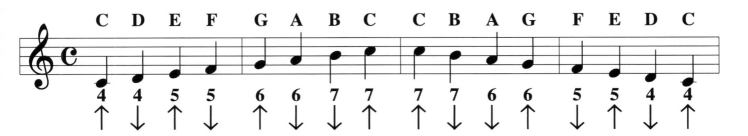

OUR FIRST SONG

Our first tune will be *Mary Had A Little Lamb*. Since almost everyone already knows this tune, it will be easy for you to tell whether you're playing it right or wrong. Work on playing single notes with a good solid tone. This means to listen for air escaping through the sides of the holes. You want to focus your air directly through each hole. We will divide this song into four parts.

PART 1

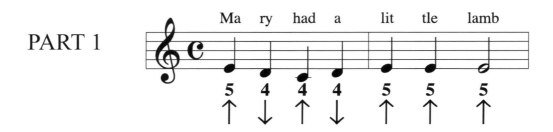

PART 2

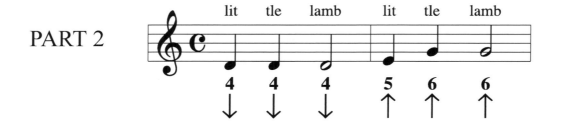

PART 3

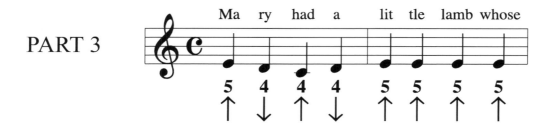

PART 4

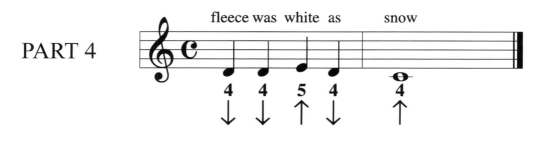

Now combine all four parts to make the complete song. Play along with the Video.

MARY HAD A LITTLE LAMB

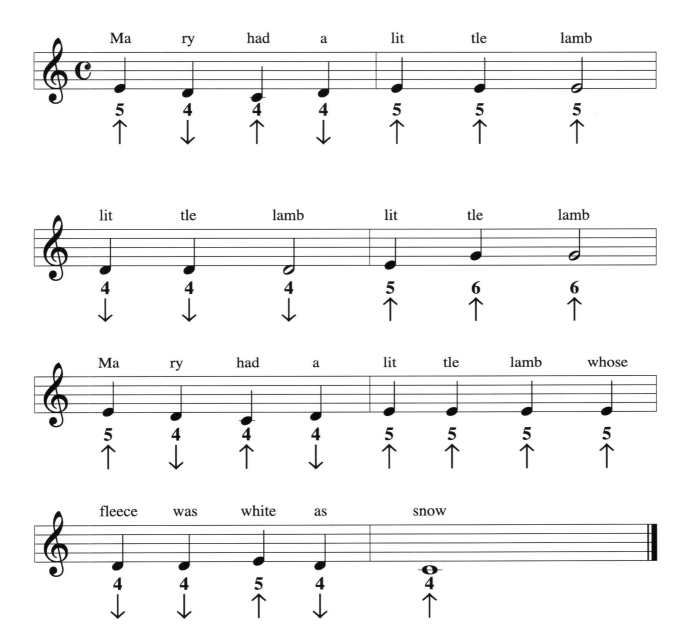

Note - All of the songs in this book are played at two speeds on the Video, slow (to practice) and up tempo (performance speed).

SONG #2

Our 2nd song is *Michael Row the Boat Ashore*. We're going to divide this song into four parts also.

PART 1

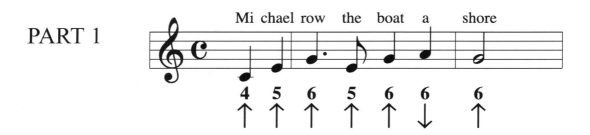

PART 2

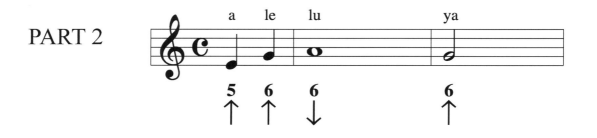

PART 3

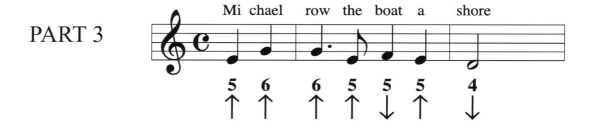

PART 4

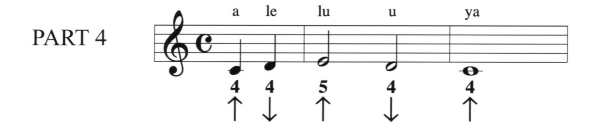

Once again, combine all four parts to play the complete song. Make sure you practice along with the Video.

MICHAEL ROW THE BOAT ASHORE

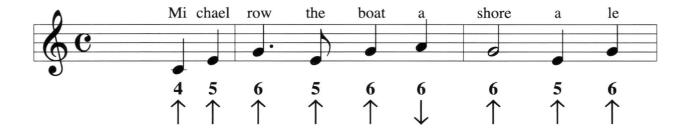

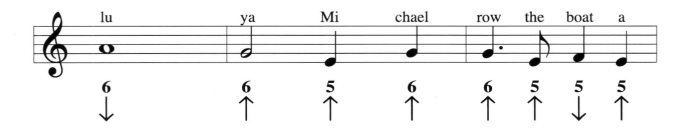

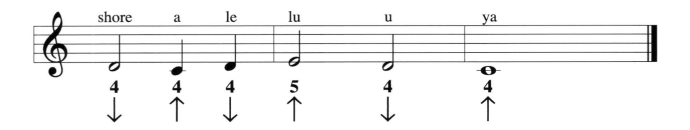

SONG #3

The next song is *London Bridge*. Again, we'll divide this song into four parts. Practice along with the Video.

PART 1

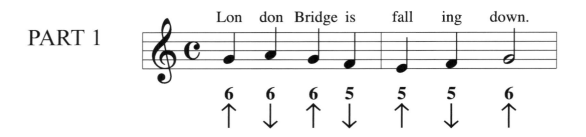

PART 2

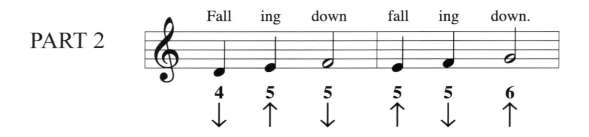

PART 3

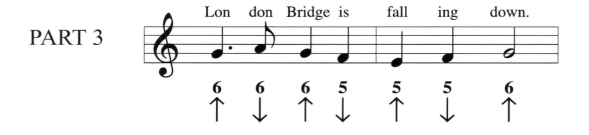

PART 4

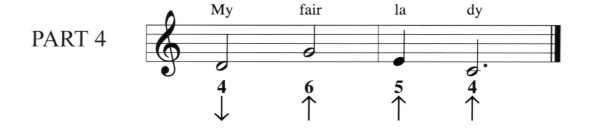

LONDON BRIDGE

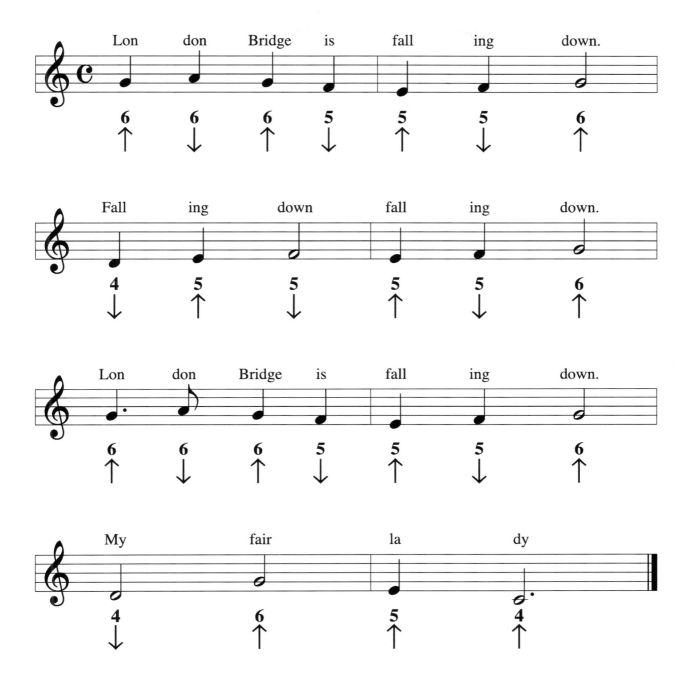

 On the next five pages you'll notice these logos. They indicate bonus songs in the book that are not on the Video. Make sure you practice these songs along with the audio tracks. You can access these tracks by going to this address on the internet:

http://cvls.com/extras/harmonica/

WILDWOOD FLOWER

STREETS OF LAREDO

RED RIVER VALLEY

THE MARINES HYMN

SECTION 3
DOUBLE STOPS

For Audio & Video Access, go to this address:
http://cvls.com/extras/harmonica/

DOUBLE STOPS

Playing two notes at a time is called a double stop. This happens quite naturally when first learning how to play. The trick is to control when you are playing more than one note at a time, and which ones you are playing. We will start by playing two notes at a time, or double stops, going up the harmonica.

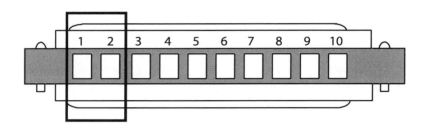

EXERCISE 6

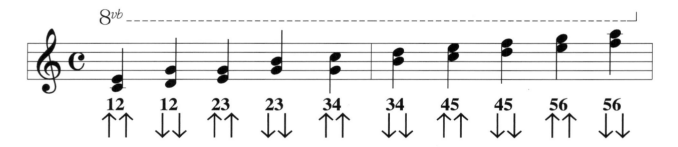

EXERCISE 7

Now come back down playing double stops.

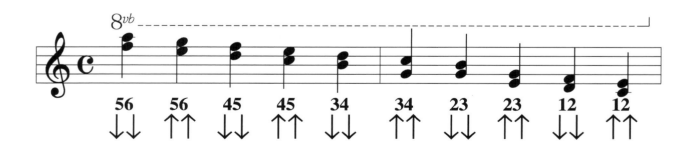

Here is a song using double stops. Play along with the Video.

GOOD NIGHT LADIES

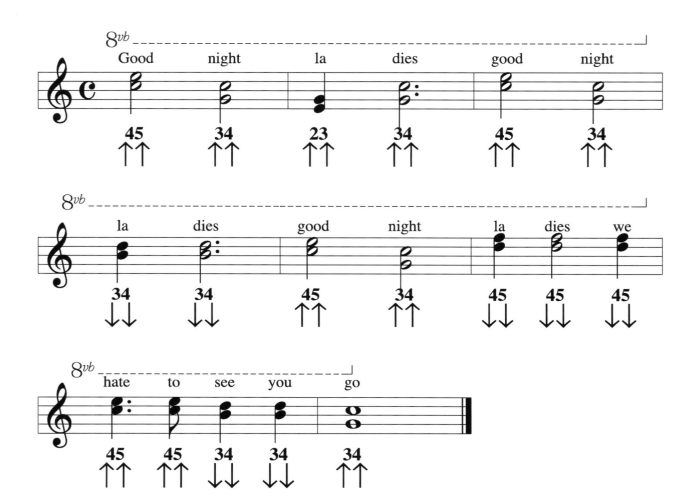

OH SUSANA

MINUET

J.S. Bach

FRERE JACQUES

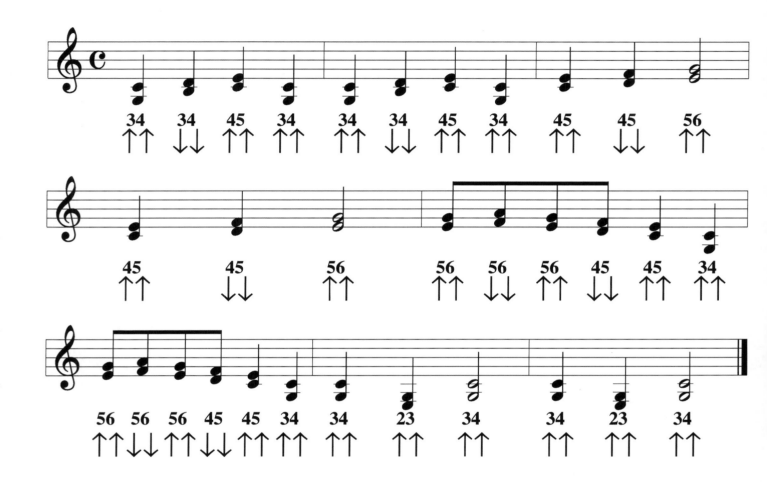

BLUES SHUFFLE

Here is a chord progression you can play on the harp called *a Blues Shuffle*. This is a great jamming tune because you can get together with friends and play along with other instruments. It is a 12 bar blues chord progression, so most musicians know it.

To play this tune, we must first learn a new technique. This technique is called "staccato" meaning short notes on the harmonica. Practice along with the Video to learn this technique.

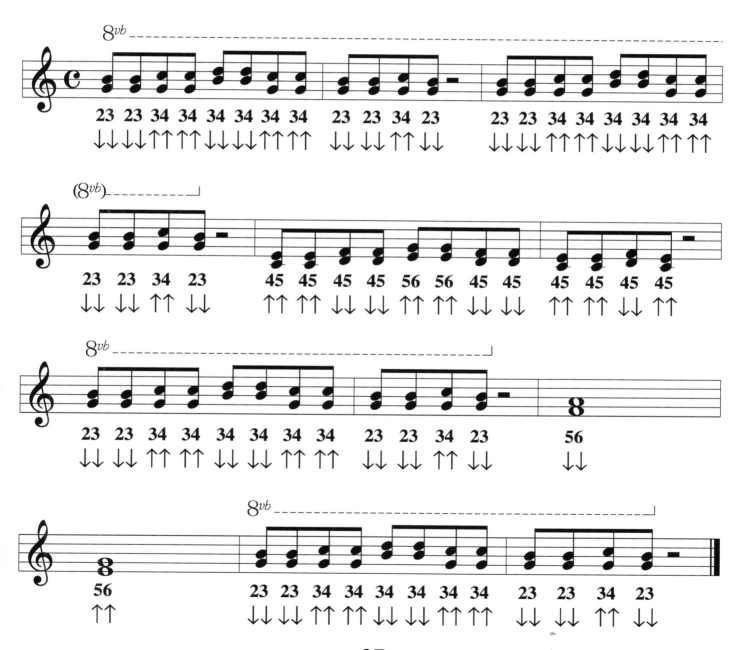

27

SECTION 4
VIBRATO

For Audio & Video Access, go to this address:
http://cvls.com/extras/harmonica/

FAN VIBRATO

To make a sweeter sound, we use a technique called vibrato, much like a singer would use. There are actually several different ways to do a vibrato on the harmonica. The first is using the left hand like a fan in front of the harmonica. What we are really doing is controlling the air flow through the harmonica. Another way to think of this is a muting effect. We stop and release air with our hand while slightly shaking the harmonica at the same time. If you are having trouble with this technique, play along with the Video..

Step 1

Start by holding the harmonica in the normal position.

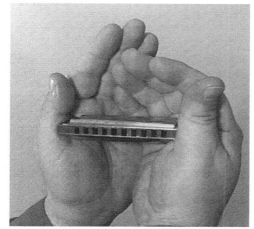

Step 2

Fan your left hand away from the harmonica. Make sure to keep your left thumb anchored in position while moving your left hand in front of the harp.

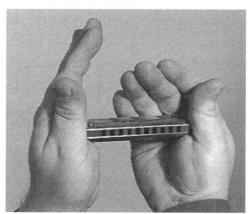

EXERCISE 8

Now let's try a vibrato together while blowing and drawing through hole 4. Listen to the Video and try to duplicate the sound.

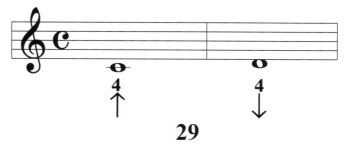

ROCKING VIBRATO

Another technique used to create a vibrato involves rocking the harmonica. We will do this with our right hand.

Step 1

Start by holding the harmonica in the normal position.

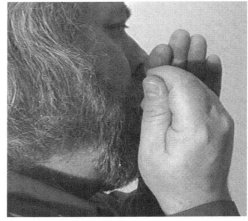

Step 2

Rock the harmonica gently back and forth with your right hand. Don't let the harmonica leave your lips. The left hand should remain stationary.

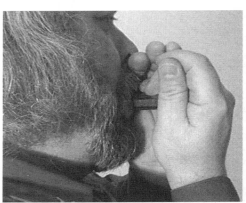

EXERCISE 9

Practice this technique while blowing and drawing through hole 3.

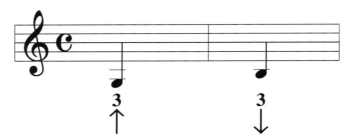

Practice this technique up and down the harmonica. Try it through all the holes while blowing and drawing. You can use either or both techniques to create vibrato. (The fan method with the left hand or the rocking method with the right hand.) Vibrato is an optional technique used for expression. It can be used anytime, usually on notes held for a while, but it is entirely up to the player when to use vibrato.

DOWN IN THE VALLEY

We will now use this effect during a song. A good song to practice vibrato is *Down in the Valley*. If you are not familiar with this song, listen to it first. Begin by practicing slowly, then speed up the tempo.

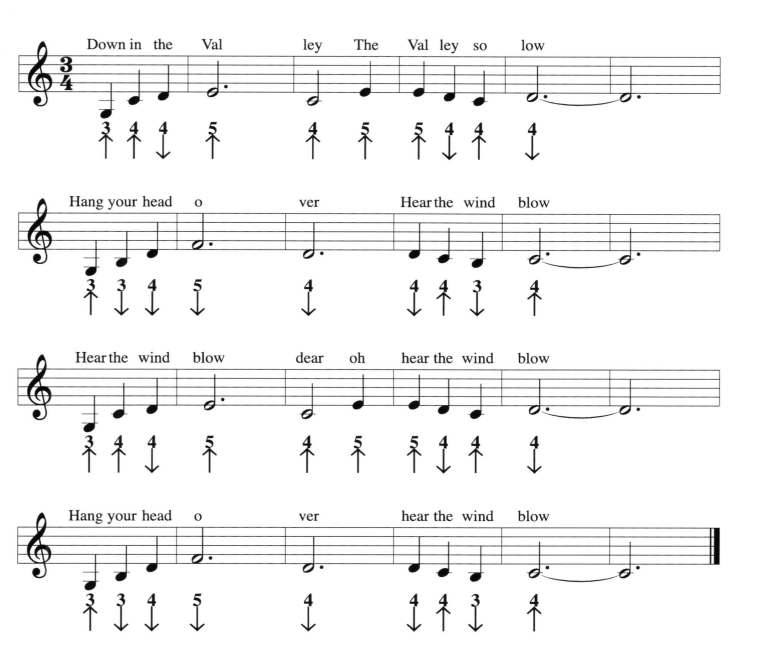

31

ON TOP OF OLD SMOKEY

AURA LEE

SILENT NIGHT

34

O CHRISTMAS TREE

JINGLE BELLS

SECTION 5
TRILLS

For Audio & Video Access, go to this address:
http://cvls.com/extras/harmonica/

TRILLS

Now we'll learn how to do a trill. This technique is executed by sliding the harmonica from side to side, playing two notes back and forth.

Step 1

Start by holding the harmonica in the normal position.

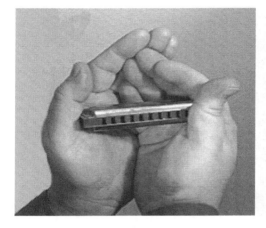

Step 2

Use the left hand as a brace or stopping point while rocking the harmonica back and forth. This also helps with keeping the harmonica in the correct position.

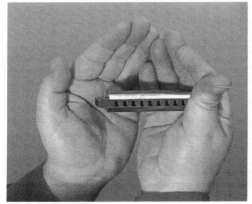

EXERCISE 10

Play a trill at the 5th and 6th holes on the harmonica, starting on hole 5 and then playing hole 6. First we will do this technique while blowing, then try the same technique while drawing. *tr = trill*

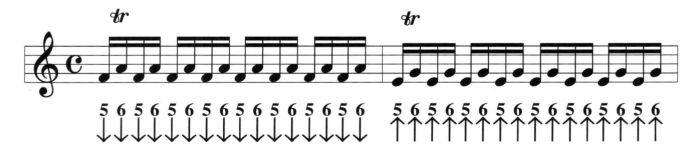

BLUES SHUFFLE (WITH TRILLS)

We will now play *A Blues Shuffle* again, but this time with trills. Practice slowly at first, then speed it up as you feel more comfortable. *tr = trill*

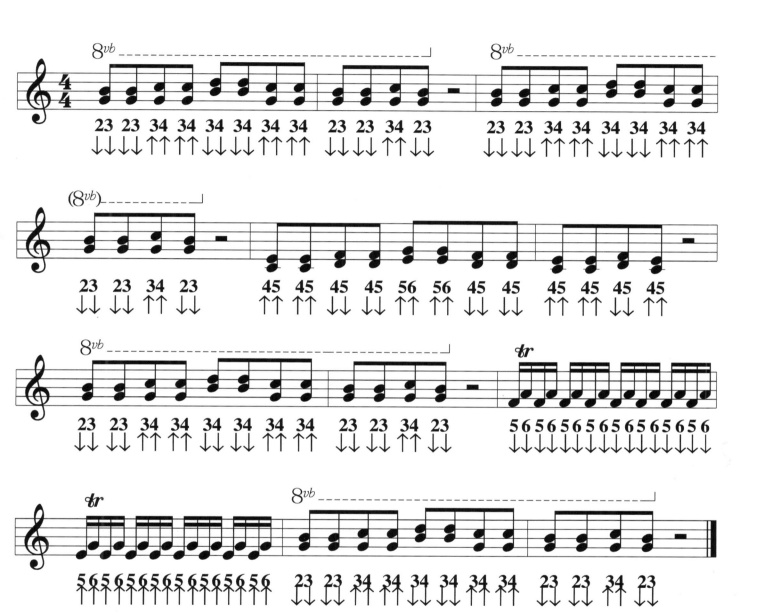

CARELESS LOVE

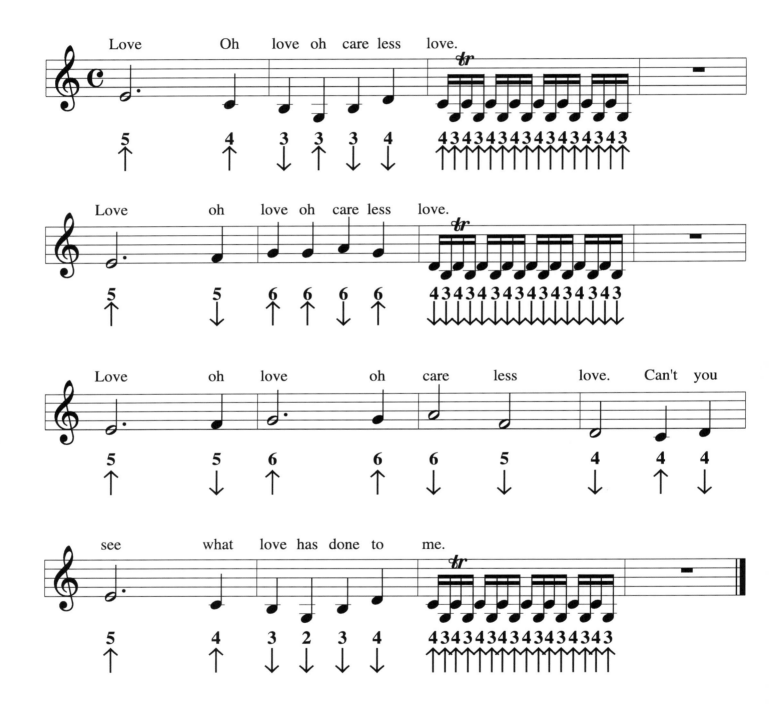

SECTION 6
CROSS HARP
or
2nd POSITION

For Audio & Video Access, go to this address:
http://cvls.com/extras/harmonica/

CROSS HARP

We are now going to learn to play in the 2nd position or what is commonly called "Cross Harp". Although we are using a C harmonica, we will actually play in the key of G. Harmonica players use this technique a great deal in order to solo or to play the blues. When you play cross harp, there are more inhale notes than exhale notes. This allows for many more expressive effects and techniques.

When you buy a harmonica, it is labeled in a certain key. Count up five letters of the musical alphabet from the harmonica key. The musical alphabet consists of A B C D E F G and then starts over again with A. There is no H, I, or J. If you are playing in the key of C, start with C and count up 5, C D E F G. G is the key you will play cross harp in. If you owned a D harmonica, you would play cross harp in the key of A - D E F G A. The A harmonica would play cross harp in the key of E - A B C D E.

Harmonica Key			Cross Harp Key	
1	2	3	4	5
C	D	E	F	G
D	E	F	G	A
E	F	G	A	B
F	G	A	B	C
G	A	B	C	D
A	B	C	D	E

THE CROSS HARP SCALE

EXERCISE 11

We will now learn a scale that is commonly used when playing cross harp. With our C harmonica we are going to play a G Major pentatonic scale.

Here's a song using the G cross harp scale on a C harmonica. Play along with the Video.

WILL THE CIRCLE BE UNBROKEN

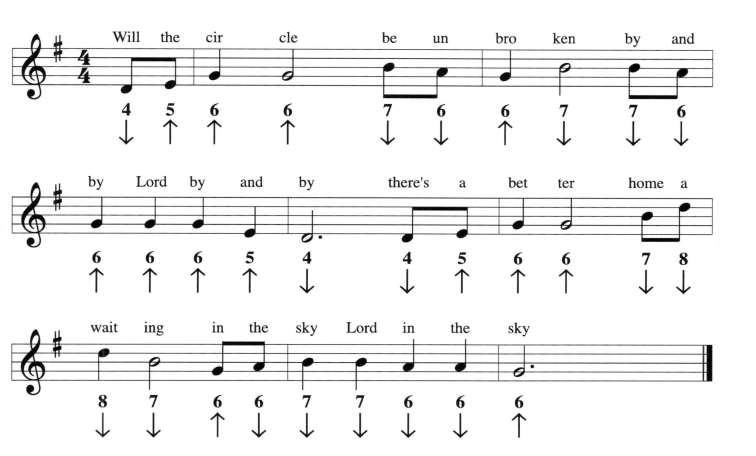

43

HARP BOOGIE

Here is another tune in the cross harp position. Remember to practice slowly at first, then speed up when you are comfortable playing it. Play along with the Video.

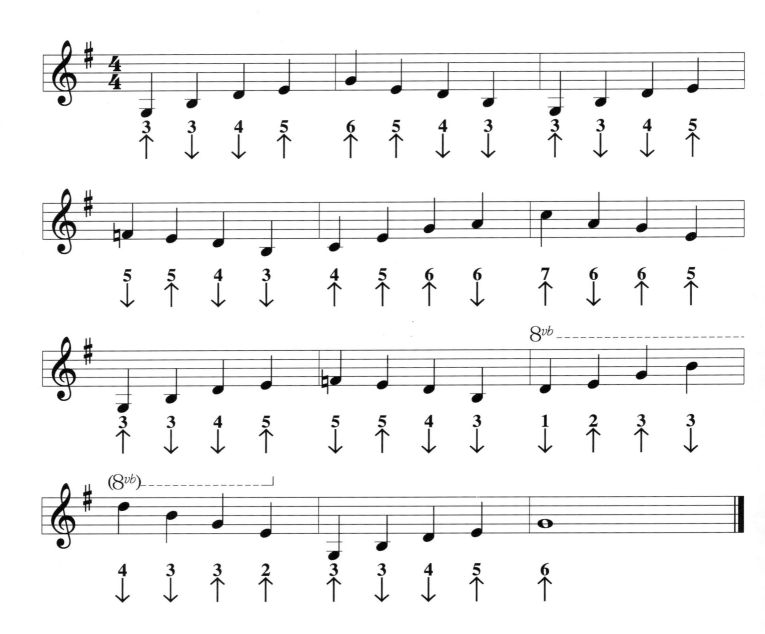

TOM DOOLEY

SECTION 7
BENDING NOTES

For Audio & Video Access, go to this address:
http://cvls.com/extras/harmonica/

BENDS

EEE

Now we will learn to bend notes. We can change the pitch of a note we are playing by forcing more air through the reed. Care must be taken here because too much force on the reed can damage it. Not all of the holes respond the same way, some notes may be bent by drawing air, some by blowing. Blowing and bending notes is an extremely advanced technique and not used by many harmonica players, so we will not use this technique. The lower register notes 1 through 6 may be bent by drawing much easier than the 7 through 10. A curved arrow will tell you this note is to be bent. Because we are always inhaling when bending notes, the arrow will always be pointing down.

Yew

4

Your hand position remains stationary for this technique. Hold your harmonica as usual. Tongue position becomes important here. Start with your tongue in the middle of your mouth. Draw air through hole 4 and make an "EEE Yew" shape with your mouth.

While making an "EEE Yew" motion, our tongue goes forward and down, and the jaw should also move forward. Remember to inhale the whole time you are making the "EEE Yew" shape. We are not actually making an "EEE Yew" sound, just the motion with our mouth and tongue. Beginners usually try to inhale too hard during this technique. Remember, finesse is required here, not force.

EXERCISE 12

We will now draw air through hole 4 and bend the note. Start by drawing normally, increasing the amount of air you are drawing, and make the EEE Yew shape with your mouth. Be patient, practice, and experiment until you can execute a bend.

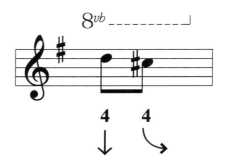

EXERCISE 13

Now let's try the same technique with hole 3.

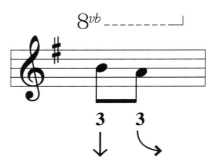

We will now learn *Amazing Grace* in the key of G, playing cross harp and bending notes. The only note we'll bend in this song is done by drawing through hole 3.

EXERCISE 14

Here is this bend in context. Notice you blow through hole 3 immediately after the bend.

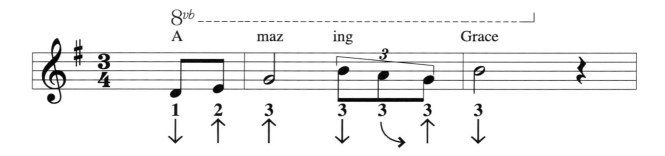

AMAZING GRACE

BASIC BLUES

In this song we'll combine many of the techniques we have learned. You will want to listen to this song once before playing. Practice the individual techniques as necessary, and then try to play them in context.

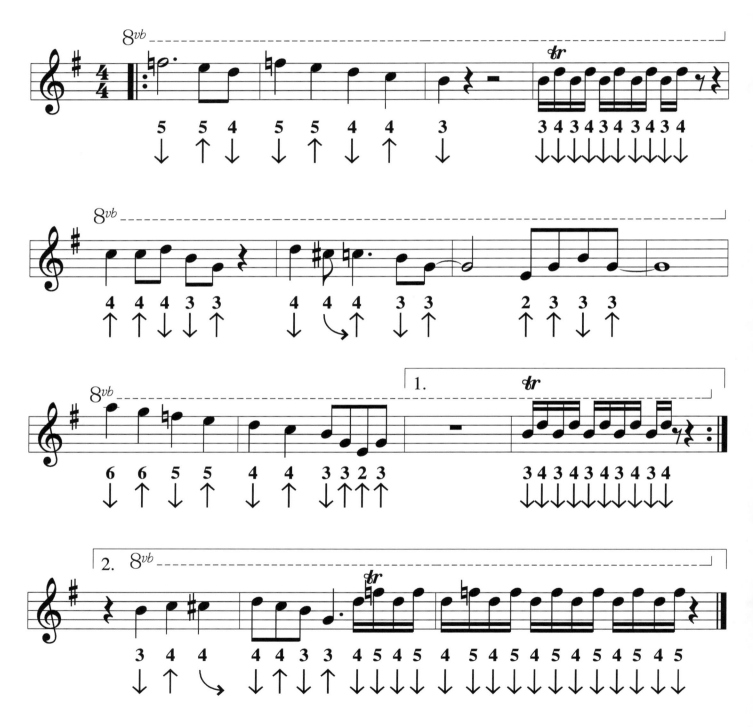

OH WHEN THE SAINTS

HE'S GOT THE WHOLE WORLD
IN HIS HANDS

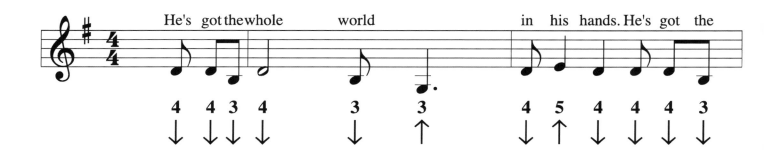

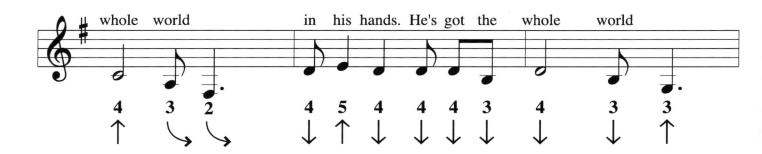

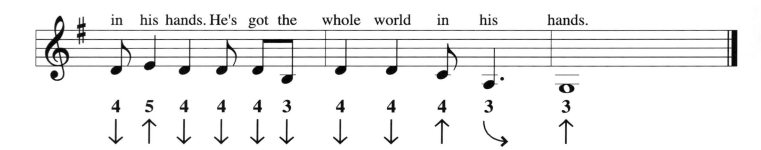

52

ROLL IN MY SWEET
BABY'S ARMS

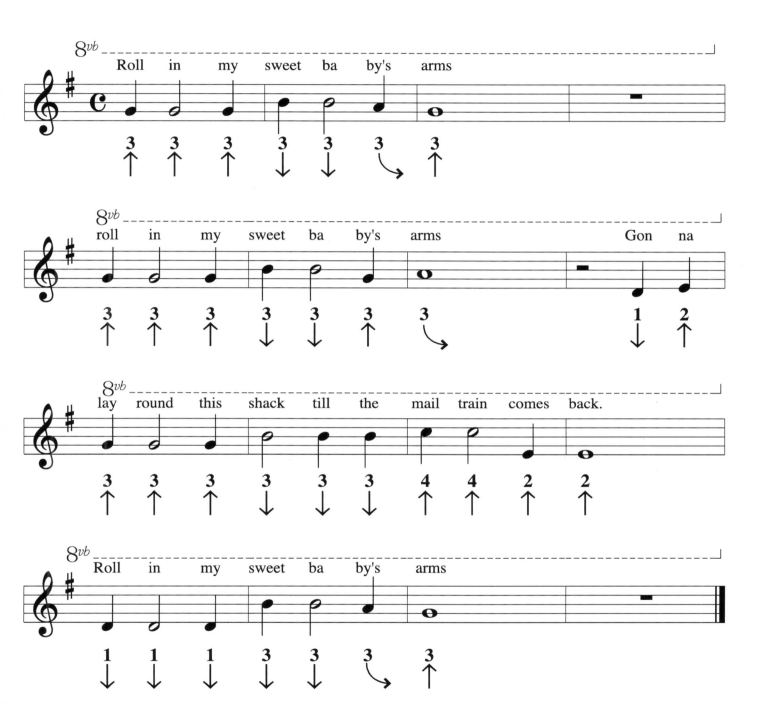

REUBEN'S TRAIN

PLAYING ALONG WITH OTHER INSTRUMENTS

For Audio & Video Access, go to this address:
http://cvls.com/extras/harmonica/

One of the reasons people enjoy playing the harmonica is the ease with which you can play with other instruments. Harmonicas come in many different keys. The one we have used during this book is in the key of C. For first position harp playing, use the same harmonica as the key of the song. If a song is in the key of A, get out an A harmonica. If a song is in the key of D, use a D harmonica. You will need harmonicas in different keys to do this and you may purchase them at your local music store quite inexpensively.

DEMONSTRATIONS

During this section we will learn how to play along with the guitar and it will be necessary to listen to the Video. There are three examples you should listen to:

	Harmonica Key	Technique
Demo 1	C	1st position
Demo 2	D	1st position
Demo 3	G	Cross Harp 2nd position

PLAYING WITH THE VIDEO

The next set of exercises involve playing along with the Video. The chart below lists the example number, the key of the harmonica, and what position to play in or what technique to use. Use this chart to play along with the Video.

This is the time to experiment. Don't try to play exactly what I'm playing, but fool around with the harmonica and develop your own melodies. In the first two examples, there are no bad notes. All of the notes on the harmonica will sound good. In the last two examples, make sure you play notes from the cross harp scale. There will be more drawing notes than blowing notes in the cross harp position.

	Harmonica Key	Technique
Example 1	C	1st Position
Example 2	C	Double stops
Example 3	C	Cross Harp 2nd position
Example 4	C	Cross Harp plus techniques

Made in the USA
Columbia, SC
05 May 2020